Lace Crochet Covered Ornaments

Six Quick and Easy Patterns with Stunning Results.

Kristen Stein

Copyright © 2019-2020 by Kristen Stein
Revised 2020.

All rights reserved. This book or any portion thereof may not be reproduced or used in any manner whatsoever without the express written permission of the author.

ISBN: 9781792939280

Contents

Pattern Notes 1

Set of 6 Designs 3

Basic Stitches & Supplies 4

Ornament Design #1 5

Ornament Design #2 7

Ornament Design #3 9

Ornament Design #4 11

Ornament Design #5 13

Ornament Design #6 15

Concluding Remarks & Other patterns 18

Other Recent Pattern Books 20

Stitch Glossary 24

About the Artist & Designer 26

Pattern Notes

This book contains six of my patterns for creating lace crochet covered ornaments. I have crocheted for many years and have created many different ornament designs. I have kept a small notebook in which I write down the patterns as they are created. This is my first attempt at publishing them for others to use. I hope the steps are easy-to-follow.

I have tried to streamline the patterns so that the ornaments can be recreated relatively quickly and easily. Experienced crocheters might notice that I do not use the conventional notation, or start each round with chain stitches to reach the "required" height. My motivation for doing so is to keep the repeated patterns short and easy to replicate. Because most stitches aren't higher than a double-crochet and because a small hook is being used, very little difference can be seen by avoiding the chain stitches at the start of each round. If you are an experienced crocheted, you can adjust the patterns to the more conventional approach to creating rounds.

The rounds are done with very basic stitches and are repeated multiple times. In most cases, I simply describe the first set of stitches and then tell the reader to "repeat around". This is for the ease of the reader in an effort to keep the instructions simple. The goal is to create rounds that are not too large, or overcrowded, so that the stitches lay nicely around a standard-sized ornament.

Most of the ornaments I used for the patterns in this book are between 60-65mm in diameter, or about 2.25-2.5 inches in diameter. If you use different-sized globe ornaments or baubles, you will need to modify the patterns to fit. This can usually be accomplished by modifying the number of rounds, or by changing the number of chain stitches in the final round of each pattern.

You can also fit the cover over the ornament at the start of the final round in order to determine if any adjustments to length are required.

I hope you find these as much fun to make as I do. They look beautiful adorned on a Christmas tree, but are equally beautiful displayed in a tabletop display with multiple baubles in contrasting patterns. These also make wonderful hostess gifts during the holidays.

Good luck and happy crafting! -Kristen

Set of 6 Designs

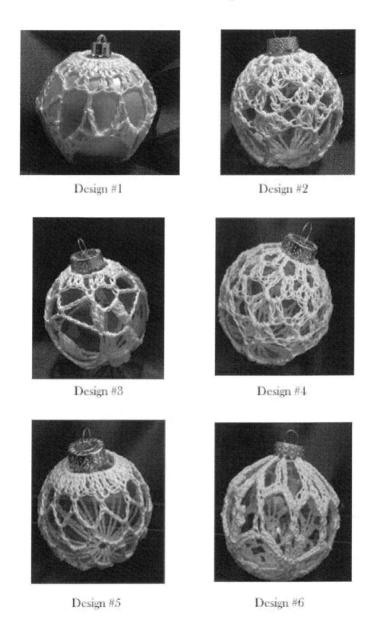

Design #1

Design #2

Design #3

Design #4

Design #5

Design #6

Basic Stitches & Supplies

Basic stitches and the abbreviations used in these six patterns. (I've included a stitch glossary in the back of the book.)

Slip-stitch
Chain stitch (ch)
Single crochet (sc)
Double-crochet (dc)
Treble-crochet (tr)
Treble-together (trtog)
Picot

Supplies needed:

Ornaments to cover. (I used glass or acrylic globe ornaments or baubles in the standard 2.25-2.5 inch diameter.)

2.5-3.0 mm crochet hook. Gauge doesn't need to be precise for this project. I generally use the 2.5mm hook and create loose stitches to allow for additional stretch if needed.

Crochet thread. I tend to use Size 10 crochet thread in white. But metallic crochet threads are beautiful as well. Experiment with colored globes with contrasting thread colors.

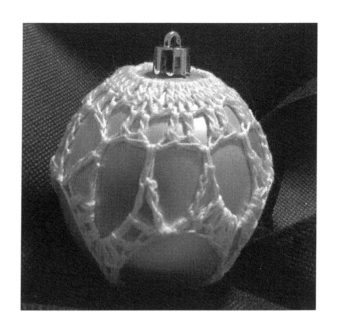

Ornament Design #1

Ch 20
Slip stitch in first chain to form a ring.

Round1 (Rd1): 36 dc into ring

Rd2: dc in each of first 2 dc; *[ch1, skip next dc, dc in each of next 2 dc] repeat from * around. On last repeat omit the 2dc. Slip stitch into first dc to end the round.

Rd3: Slip stitch in first ch1 space. Ch9, *[slip stitch into next ch1 space, ch9] repeat from * around. Slip stitch in the base of the first ch9 to end the round. (You should have twelve ch9 loops.)

Rd4: (4dc, ch5,4dc) in first ch9 loop, slip stitch in next ch9 loop, *[(4dc, ch5,4dc) in next ch9 loop, slip stitch in next ch9 loop] repeat from * around ending with a slip stitch in the first dc to end the round. (You should have six ch5 spaces.)

Rd5: Slip stitch across the first dc's in order to start the round in the first ch5 space. *[Ch15, slip stitch into next ch5 space] repeat from * around. End round with a slip stitch into the base of the first ch15. (You should have six ch15 loops.)

Fasten off. Weave in ends.

Cut 10-12 inch piece of crochet thread. Fit crochet design over the globe ornament or bauble. Weave the thread through each of the ch15 loops. Pull to gather the loops at the bottom of the globe. (Or at the top, depending on how you positioned the cover.)

Tie a knot to secure the gathered loops. Trim and weave in the ends.

Ornament Design #2

Ch 20
Slip stitch in first chain to form a ring.

Rd1: (2dc, ch2) into ring 9 times. Slip stitch in first dc to end round. You should end with 9 ch2 spaces.

Rd2: Slip stitch in first ch2 space to start the round. (2dc, ch2, 2dc) in each ch2 space around. Slip stitch in opening stitch to end round. You should have nine ch2 spaces.

Rd3-4: Repeat Rd2. You should still have nine ch2 spaces.

Rd5: Slip stitch in first ch2 space, *[ch9, sc in next ch2 space] repeat from * around. End with a slip stitch in base of first ch9 loop. You should end with nine ch9 loops.

Rd6: Slip stitch across to the center of the first ch9 loop to start the round. 2sc into loop, *[ch12, 2sc in next ch9 loop] repeat from * around. End with slip stitch into first sc. you should end with nine ch12 loops.

Fasten off. Weave in ends.

Cut 10 inch piece of thread. Weave through the nine ch12 loops. Position the crochet design over the bauble. Pull thread to gather loops. Tie a knot. Trim and weave in ends.

Ornament Design #3

Ch 20
Slip stitch in first chain to form a ring.

Rd1: (3tr, ch2) into ring 8 times. Slip stitch in starting stitch to end round. You should end with 8 ch2 spaces.

Rd2: slip stitch in first ch2 space. (Ch6, sc) in each ch2 space around. Slip stitch in starting stitch to end round. (You should end with 8 ch6 loops)

Rd3: *[(3trtog, ch3, 3trtog) in ch6 loop, (ch3, sc, ch3) in next ch6 loop] repeat from * around. Slip stitch in starting stitch to end round. You should have four ch3 spaces between trtog clusters.

Rd4: Slip stitch into the ch3 space between the trtog clusters to start the round. [(3trtog, ch3, 3trtog), ch6] in each ch3 between trtog clusters around. On final repeat, omit the last ch6. Instead do ch3 and tr into starting chain to mimic the last ch6 space. This combination of (ch3+tr) will mimic the last ch-6 space, but place us in the center of the last loop to start the next round.

Rd5: *[Ch15, (3trtog, ch3, 3trtog) in ch3 space between trtog clusters, ch15, sc in ch6 space] repeat from * around. End with slip stitch in base of starting ch15. You should end with eight ch15 loops.

Fasten off. Weave in ends.

Cut 10-12 inch piece of crochet thread. Fit crochet design over the globe ornament or bauble. Weave the thread through each of the ch15 loops. Pull to gather the loops at the bottom of the globe. (Or at the top, depending on how you positioned the cover.)

Tie a knot to secure the gathered loops. Trim and weave in the ends.

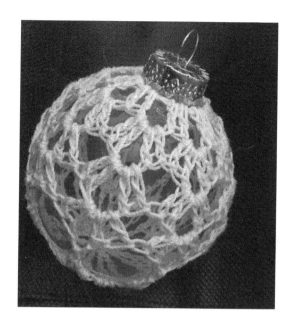

Ornament Design #4

Ch 18
Slip stitch in first chain to form a ring.

Rd1: (2dc, ch2) into ring 9 times on final repeat omit ch2 and instead do ch 1 and sc in first dc to start in the center of the last ch2 space of round. You should have a total of 9 ch2 spaces.

Rd2: 2dc in starting space, (2dc, ch2, 2dc) in each ch2 space around. On final repeat do 2dc in opening ch2 space and instead of a ch2 do ch1 and sc to first dc. This will create the final ch2 space, but start us in the center for the next round.

End with nine ch2 spaces.

Rds3-4: Repeat Rd2 two more times. You should still have 9 ch2 spaces.

Rd5: *[Ch9, sc in next ch2 space] Repeat from * around. End with a slip stitch in base of first ch9. You should have 9 ch9 loops.

Rd6: (2dc, ch9, 2dc) into each ch9 loop around. End with a slip stitch in starting stitch.

Fasten off. Weave in ends.

Cut 10-12 inch piece of crochet thread. Fit crochet design over the globe ornament or bauble. Weave the thread through each of the ch9 loops. Pull to gather the loops at the bottom of the globe. (Or at the top, depending on how you positioned the cover.)

Tie a knot to secure the gathered loops. Trim and weave in the ends.

Ornament Design #5

Ch 20
Slip stitch in first chain to form a ring.

Rd1: 36dc into ring. Slip stitch in starting dc to end round.

Rd2: Sc in starting dc, *[ch5, skip 2dc, sc in next dc] repeat from * around. On last repeat omit the ch5 and do a ch3 and dc into opening sc to start the next round in the center of the last ch5 loop. The combination of a (ch3+dc) will mimic the last ch-5 space, but allow us to end in the center of the space for the next round. You should have 12 ch5 spaces.

Rd3: Sc in opening space, *[ch5, sc in next ch5 space] repeat from * around. On final repeat, omit ch5 and do a ch3, dc in starting sc to start us in the center of last ch5 space. Still 12 ch5 spaces.

Rd4: *[Ch7, 3sc in next ch5 loop] repeat from * around, ending with 3sc in starting loop. Slip stitch in base of first ch7. You should have 12 ch7 loops.

Rd5: Slip stitch in the center of the ch7 loop. (Or, if you prefer, you can fasten off at the end of around 4 and then start Round 5 from the center of the ch7 loop.) *[Ch18, 3sc in next ch7 loop] Repeat from * around ending with 3sc in starting loop.
Slip stitch in base of initial ch18 to end the round.
End with 12 ch18 loops.

Fasten off. Weave in ends.

Cut 10-12 inch piece of crochet thread. Fit crochet design over the globe ornament or bauble. Weave the thread through each of the ch18 loops. Pull to gather the loops at the bottom of the globe. (Or at the top, depending on how you positioned the cover.)

Tie a knot to secure the gathered loops. Trim and weave in the ends.

Ornament Design #6

(Note: This design starts with a smaller ring. It is intended to be designed from the "bottom up" with the loops gathered at the top of the bauble. If you choose to do this as a "top down" design, you'll need to choose an opening ring that covers the ornaments hanger on the top.)

Ch6
Slip stitch in first chain to form a ring.

Rd1: (2dc, ch1) six times into ring. Slip stitch in first dc to end round. End with six 2dc and six ch1 spaces.

Rd2: Slip stitch in first ch1 space. (2dc, ch1, 2dc) in each ch1 space around. Slip stitch into first dc to end the round. You should have six ch1 spaces.

Rd3: Slip stitch in first ch1 space to start the round. (2dc, ch1,2dc) in first ch1 space, *[ch5, (2dc,ch1,2dc) in next ch1 space] repeat from * around. End with ch5 and slip stitch in first dc. You should have six ch5 spaces and six ch1 spaces.

Rd4: Slip stitch in first ch1 space to start the round. (2dc, ch1,2dc) in first ch1 space, *[ch5, slip stitch in ch5 space, ch5, (2dc,ch1,2dc) in next ch1 space] repeat from * around. End with ch5 and slip stitch in first dc. You should have six ch1 spaces. (You'll also have 12 ch5 spaces, but we won't be stitching into those on the next round.)

Rd5: In this round, we will only be working in the ch1 spaces. Slip stitch into first ch1 space. (2dc, ch1,2dc) in first ch1 space, *[ch9, (2dc, ch1,2dc) in next ch1 space] repeat from * around. On final repeat ch9 and slip stitch into top of first dc. You should have six ch9 spaces and six ch1 spaces.

Rd6: Slip stitch in first ch1 space. (Ch3, 3picot,ch3, sc) in same ch1 space, *[(4sc, ch6, 4sc) in ch9 space, slip stitch in next ch1 space, (Ch3, 3picot,ch3, sc) in same ch1 space] repeat from * around. End final repeat with the 4sc in last ch9 space. Slip stitch in base of first ch3 to end round.

You should finish the round with six ch6 loops and six 3picot loops. Fasten off.

Rd7: Reconnect thread in top of the second picot in the first set of 3picots. *[ch6, slip stitch into next ch6 space, ch6, slip stitch into top of second picot] repeat from * around. End with a slip stitch in base of opening ch6. You should have 12 ch6 spaces.

Rd8: (4sc, ch15, 4sc) in each ch6 space around. Slip stitch in opening stitch to end the round.

Fasten off. Weave in ends.

Cut 10-12 inch piece of crochet thread. Fit crochet design over the globe ornament or bauble. Weave the thread through each of the ch15 loops. Pull to gather the loops at the top of the globe.

Tie a knot to secure the gathered loops. Trim and weave in the ends.

Concluding Remarks & Other patterns

Congratulations on completely your 6 "Lace Crochet Covered Ornaments". See my other patterns for the "Large Lace Covered Ornaments" that include a set of patterns to cover large 4" diameter globes. These look great displayed on a tree as above, or made with many different size and colors of ornamental balls, globes, rocks, pebbles and more. They can certainly adorn the tree or tables during holidays, but can be made for weddings, Easter baskets, or other special occasion. You can even choose to wrap your favorite stone or pebble from a from a special trip or vacation destination. Try different sized baubles and experiment with what works best for you. I hope you enjoyed these patterns. Please take a look at my other pattern books for crocheted garments and accessories.

Try different sized baubles. See my other patterns for the the larger globe designs.

Other Recent Pattern Books

Most recently added:

Available as eBooks or Paperbacks Learn more about these titles on my blog: http://kristensteinfineart.blogspot.com
or search Amazon & Ravelry for Kristen Stein.

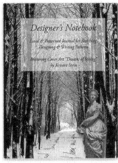

Additional sketch and design books are also available. Visit my Amazon author page or blog for more information.

Photo 52: Designer Sketchbooks.

New line of sketchbook and design books to aid in the design process for fashion designers, especially those that knit, crochet, sew or quilt. The designer's notebooks have both lined and patterned pages to provide an area to sketch out the design and an area to write pattern notes.

Stitch Glossary

Bobble or Cluster – See **"Treble-Crochet-Together Cluster/Bobble"** below.

Chain stitch (ch) - Start with a slipknot. Insert your crochet hook through the slipknot then pick up the yarn with the hook. Pull the yarn through the slip knot back to front. This is the first chain stitch.

Double-crochet (dc) - Yarn over the hook, insert hook into the next stitch to be worked and yarn over again. Pull the yarn through the stitch and yarn over again. You should now have three loops on the hook. Pull the yarn through both loops and yarn over again. Pull yarn through the last two loops on the hook to complete the double crochet.

Double-Crochet Together (specifically dc2tog): Often used to easily decrease stitches by combining two dc stitches into one dc stitch. Yarn over. Insert hook into next stitch. Yarn over. Pull yarn through stitch. You should have three stitches on hook. Yarn over. Pull yarn through first two loops on hook. You should now have two loops on hook. Yarn over. Insert hook in next stitch. Yarn over. Pull yarn through stitch. You should have four loops on hook. Yarn over. Pull through first two loops. Yarn over. Pull yarn through all three loops on hook.

Half-Double-Crochet (hdc) – Similar to a double-crochet, but it ends up with a slightly shorter stitch. Yarn over the hook, insert hook into the next stitch to be worked and yarn over again. Pull the yarn through the stitch and yarn over again. You should now have three loops on the hook. Pull the yarn all three loops to complete the half-double crochet.

Picot (p) – The picot is a decorative stitch that is often used in borders or trim to add a little extra charm or flourish to the final project. The most common picot is the ch3 or ch4 picot. My patterns use the ch3 picot (unless otherwise noted). To create a ch3 picot, simply ch3 and then insert your hook in the third chain from hook. Yarn over and pull through the stitch and through the loop on the hook. Basically, you ch3 and then slip stitch into the first chain of the ch3. This will create a tight little "dot" that adds a nice decorative trim to the final piece.

Single Crochet (sc) - Insert the hook into stitch. Yarnover and pull the yarn through the loop on your hook. Yarn over again and pull the yarn through both loops on your hook. You've created one single crochet stitch.

Slip stitch (sl st) - Slip stitches are convenient for transitioning between rounds and helping to move the yarn or thread to different starting positions without adding height or bulk. To make a slip stitch, insert your hook through the desired space. Hook your yarn and pull it through. You've just made your first slip stitch.

Treble crochet (tr) - Also called a triple crochet. Yarn over your hook twice. Insert the hook into the next stitch. Yarn over and draw the yarn through the stitch. You should have four loops on the hook. Yarn over the hook again and draw the yarn through two of the four loops on the hook. Yarn over again and draw through two more loops. Yarn over again and draw through last two loops. You should be left with one loop on hook to start next stitch.

Treble-Crochet-Together Cluster/Bobble ('trtog cluster/bobble") – This stitch creates a cluster of treble crochets all sharing the same stitch space when complete. *Yarn over twice, insert your hook into stitch, yarn over and pull up a loop. Yarn over and draw through 2 loops. Yarn over and draw through two loops again. Yarn over twice, insert hook in same stitch, yarn over and pull up a loop, yarn over and draw through two loops, yarn over and draw through 2 loops (you should now have 3 loops on hook.) **

For a **tr2tog**, yarn over and draw through the last 3 loops on the hook to complete the tr2tog.

For a **tr3tog,** do * to ** as described above, but to create the third trtog, you will need to yarn over twice, insert the hook into designated stitch again and then yarn over and draw up a loop, yarn over and draw through 2 loops, yarn over and draw through 2 more loops, (you'll have 4 loops on the hook), yarn over and draw through all 4 loops on the hook. You have now created a **tr3tog cluster/bobble.**

About the Artist & Designer

Kristen Stein is an award-winning Contemporary Artist living in Suburban Philadelphia. Kristen's works are currently available on a variety of online venues and boutiques and galleries throughout the US. Her art has appeared in numerous printed media including posters, books, CD Covers, calendars and program covers. Her work has been licensed for use on gift items, household goods, puzzles and jewelry items. Her work has appeared in a number of solo and group exhibitions and in the set design for various television shows and a major motion picture. Although the bulk of her portfolio focuses on her original paintings and designs, Kristen also enjoys needlework and creating her own original crochet patterns. A self-proclaimed "espresso aficionado", Kristen is still trying to master the latte art technique. Although, nowhere near perfecting the technique, she still enjoys every delicious attempt.

Please visit http://kristensteinfineart.blogspot.com or http://StudioArtworks.com for more information.

On Instagram: kristensteindesigns.

Made in the USA
Middletown, DE
02 September 2024

60204636R00021